VEGAN
SNACKS

SIMPLE, DELICIOUS SWEET AND SAVOURY TREATS

summersdale

VEGAN SNACKS

An Hachette UK Company
www.hachette.co.uk

Summersdale Publishers Ltd
Part of Octopus Publishing Group Limited
Carmelite House
50 Victoria Embankment
LONDON
EC4Y 0DZ
UK

www.summersdale.com

Printed and bound in China

ISBN: 978-1-78685-970-9

Substantial discounts on bulk quantities of Summersdale books are available to corporations, professional associations and other organisations. For details contact general enquiries: telephone: +44 (0) 1243 771107 or email: enquiries@summersdale.com.

CONTENTS

Introduction

Vegan has never been more in vogue! Whether you are a seasoned plant-based cook or just starting to reduce the amount of animal products you eat, this book is for you. From simple to sumptuous, savoury to sweet, the recipes collected here offer something for everyone. There are delicious 'light bites' to try for breakfast, energy-dense, superfood-rich bars, balls and bakes, and sumptuous shakes – not to mention those all-important cakes!

The reasons for going vegan (or for reducing the amount of animal products in your diet) are numerous, including a host of health benefits such as reduced cholesterol, higher fibre intake, and making it easier to get your five a day. Whether this choice is for your health, for the animals, or for the planet, the recipes in this book are nutritious and a wonderful addition to a balanced diet. I hope you enjoy making and eating them as much as I enjoyed creating them!

NB Oven temperatures are for regular ovens – adjust for fan ovens accordingly.

Note on ingredients

While some of you might be long-term vegans, for others this might be the first time you're trying out vegan recipes – hopefully the recipes themselves will prove simple to follow, but as a help, here are a few tips on ingredients.

Most of the recipes here use whole, natural vegan foods. Some of the sweeter recipes use maple syrup or agave nectar, where you might see honey in a non-vegan version, and others use fresh or dried fruit to sweeten them. In baked goods, eggs can be replaced a number of ways, such as with a flax egg (ground flax seeds mixed with water) or with apple puree or mashed banana. One of the best things to do is to try different combinations and see what works best for you – if you try a cake recipe that suggests a flax egg, but you want a sponge that is more moist, perhaps try apple puree instead.

One of the common mistakes people make when they hear 'vegan' is assuming that everything is also gluten-free. Whilst many of the recipes here are gluten-free, if you wish to make other recipes gluten-free, this can be easily done. For the toasts, choose a vegan, gluten-free sourdough. For the bakes that contain flour, there are now many easily-substituted gluten-free flour blends. You may need to add xanthan gum for stability – this is easy to find in supermarkets and health food shops.

Lastly, if there is an ingredient you don't usually enjoy, I would urge you to try it as sometimes a new combination can change your opinion on something – like an avocado, for instance. But remember, you are cooking for *you*, and cooking should be enjoyable – substituting for a favourite ingredient – like switching strawberries for raspberries in your morning smoothie – makes the recipe more yours. So go on, dive in and experiment!

BREAKFAST BARS AND MORNING PICK-ME-UPS

Cacao granola bites • Chia pudding with berries • Breakfast smoothies • Frozen berry and oat smoothie • Energy balls • Acai smoothie bowl • Nutty granola energy bars • Fruity overnight oat breakfast bowl • Breakfast toast toppings • Granola jar

CACAO GRANOLA BITES

Delicious, nutritious, and easy to make, these gorgeous nibbles are perfect for breakfast on the go.

Method

In a large bowl, mix together the oats, pumpkin seeds, cacao powder and chocolate chips. Add the coconut oil (you may need to soften it slightly in your hands) and the maple syrup, and mix.

Add the vanilla extract and mix until fully combined – the mixture should be a little sticky.

Using your palms, roll the mixture into balls. Roll in the toasted oats, then refrigerate for 1 to 2 hours until set.

Makes

12 bites

Ingredients

100 g whole oats
50 g pumpkin seeds
4 tbsp cacao powder
1 handful of dark
    chocolate chips
3 tbsp coconut oil
3 tbsp maple syrup
1.5 tsp vanilla extract
toasted oats, for rolling

CHIA PUDDING WITH BERRIES

Chia pudding is great to make the evening before and chill overnight, so it's ready to eat first thing when you wake. If berries aren't your thing, try substituting your favourite fruit.

Method

Mix together the chia seeds, coconut milk and vanilla. Let the mixture sit for a few minutes, then stir to prevent the seeds from clumping together. Taste and add agave if you would like. Refrigerate overnight to fully set.

In the morning, rinse some blueberries and chop some fresh strawberries to top. As an optional extra, you could add a couple of tablespoons of vanilla or almond soya yoghurt as another layer between the chia pudding and the berries.

Makes

2 servings

Ingredients

6 tbsp black chia seeds
475 ml coconut milk
1 tsp vanilla extract
agave nectar, to taste
strawberries and
    blueberries, to top

BREAKFAST SMOOTHIES

A fantastic quick fix, smoothies give you a couple of your five a day, and are completely customisable to your own tastes. Try these three suggestions and see where your taste buds take you next!

Method

Wash, peel and chop your chosen fruit. Put the ingredients into a blender or smoothie maker and pulse until smooth. Add more ice for a cooler/thicker drink, and more liquid for a thinner one.

To save time on the preparation, frozen fruit works very well in a smoothie. Wash, peel, chop and freeze your fruit ahead of time – just omit the ice cubes when you make your smoothie.

Makes

Each variation makes 1 large smoothie

Ingredients

250 ml apple juice
ice cubes

For mango:
1 fresh mango

For kiwi-lime:
2 kiwi fruits
juice of ½ a lime
½ green apple, chopped

For berry-grape:
1 handful of blueberries
and 1 handful
of raspberries
10 strawberries
10 black or red
seedless grapes

FROZEN BERRY AND OAT SMOOTHIE

Make more of a meal out of your smoothie with the energy-dense oats in this complete breakfast in a glass. You can freeze your own berries or buy a ready-frozen mixed-berry selection – either will work well.

Method

Place all the ingredients except the garnish into a blender or smoothie maker and pulse until smooth. Add more oats for a denser drink, or more liquid for a lighter one.

Makes

1 glass

Ingredients

2 handfuls of frozen
    mixed berries (such
    as blueberries,
    raspberries,
    strawberries and
    redcurrants), plus
    extra to garnish
400 ml apple juice
2 tbsp whole oats
pumpkin seeds,
    to garnish

ENERGY BALLS

Cranberries and dates work in beautiful balance in these decadent-tasting bliss balls.

Method

Soak the dates in warm water for 10 minutes.

Put all the ingredients into your blender or food processor, then blitz until the mixture begins to combine – you want a few larger pieces for texture.

Using your palms, roll the mixture into balls of even size.

Leave to set for at least 2 hours before enjoying with your morning coffee.

Makes

Around 15 balls

Ingredients

175 g dates
100 g whole almonds
70 g walnuts
75 g dried cranberries
1 tbsp coconut oil

ACAI SMOOTHIE BOWL

Enriched with superfood acai berries, this rich and fruity smoothie bowl is a great boost first thing in the morning.

Method

Wash, de-stalk and chop the strawberries, wash the blueberries and raspberries.

Put all the ingredients except the garnish into your blender or smoothie maker, and pulse until smooth. The acai berries and flax seeds will mean this may need longer than your standard smoothie, and you are looking for a thicker consistency than your morning smoothie drink.

Pour the mixture into 2 bowls. Top with a sprinkling of garnishes of your choice – coconut flakes and pumpkin seeds add a lovely crunch, but whatever fruits, nuts or seeds you have to hand will work too!

Makes

2 bowls

Ingredients

20 fresh strawberries
1 handful of fresh
    blueberries
2 handfuls of fresh
    raspberries
2 tbsp dried acai berries
    or acai powder
2 tbsp ground flax seeds
4 tbsp almond
    soya yoghurt
300 ml apple juice
your choice of seeds,
    coconut flakes, mint,
    nuts, berries or other
    fruit, to garnish

NUTTY GRANOLA ENERGY BARS

Packed full of nutritious nuts and seeds, these flapjack-esque bars are full of slow-release energy to fuel your day.

Method

Take a shallow baking tin and either line with greaseproof paper or lightly grease with coconut oil.

Mix all the dry ingredients together in a large bowl.

In a saucepan, gently heat the almond butter and maple syrup, then pour over the oat mixture and mix thoroughly.

Transfer to your baking tin. Press down very firmly so that they hold their shape when cut.

Chill for at least 20 minutes, then turn out from the dish and cut into bars.

Makes

Around 10 bars

Ingredients

200 g oats
100 g dried cranberries
75 g poppy seeds
100 g whole almonds
50 g sunflower seeds
3 tbsp ground
    flax seeds
4 tbsp almond butter
5 tbsp maple syrup

FRUITY OVERNIGHT OAT BREAKFAST BOWL

Overnight oats are one of the simplest ways to have a high-energy, healthy breakfast that's ready to go when you are. Faster first thing than porridge, and fewer pans to wash too!

Method

The evening before you want to enjoy your oats, mix together the oats and soya milk in a bowl or jar – you can add a little sweetener such as agave nectar, to taste, if you prefer it sweeter. Leave in the fridge overnight.

In the morning, prepare the fruit by washing, peeling and slicing as necessary, and arrange on top of the oats. Sprinkle with the poppy seeds.

Makes

1 bowl – double up on ingredients to make 2

Ingredients

60 g oats
235 ml soya milk
agave nectar, to taste
1 banana
1 kiwi
1 handful of
    blueberries
1 handful of washed
    strawberries
poppy seeds, to garnish

BREAKFAST TOAST TOPPINGS

Toast is such a staple for breakfast that you might believe it to be boring. But with these deliciously different combinations, you'll fall back in love with toast in no time! Try them all, or just try one – they're great to mix and match.

Method

Toast the bread according to taste.

If you opt for one of the cream cheese bases, spread liberally with your choice of vegan cream cheese and top with either sliced figs and halved blackberries, halved cherry tomatoes and cress, or sliced sharon fruit and pomegranate seeds.

And for the classic peanut butter toast, spread liberally and then top with slices of banana and a sprinkling of chopped pecans.

Makes

As many servings as desired — simply make more slices

Ingredients

bread for toasting —
I suggest sourdough,
or a gluten-free
sourdough alternative
vegan cream cheese
figs
blackberries
cherry tomatoes
cress
sharon fruit
pomegranate seeds
smooth natural
peanut butter
banana
chopped pecan nuts

GRANOLA JAR

This is a cheeky cheat – choose your favourite granola and layer with fresh fruit and soya yoghurt for a quick and nutritious breakfast.

Method

Prepare the fruit by washing, peeling and chopping as necessary.

Layer the granola, fruit and yoghurt in even layers in a glass or jar, finishing with a layer of fruit on the top.

Makes

As many as desired – simply portion out the granola and toppings per person.

Ingredients

granola of choice
fresh fruit, such as
    strawberries,
    blueberries, kiwi
    and pineapple
soya yoghurt –
    I recommend
    strawberry or
    almond

DIPS AND NIBBLES

Hummus • Herbed falafel • Guacamole
• Pesto • Root vegetable crisps • Kale
crisps • Lemon and thyme sweet potato
crisps • Caramel popcorn • Homemade
oven-dried mango • Fruit leather •
Cinnamon and maple-roasted walnuts
• Salt and pepper roasted chickpeas

HUMMUS

A Middle Eastern classic, hummus is a protein-packed powerhouse and cornerstone of vegan cookery. This smooth hummus is slightly spicy, and is fantastic when paired with flatbreads, used as a spread in sandwiches, or as a dip.

Method

Simply place the ingredients into your food processor and blitz. Add a little water to thin if necessary, and blitz again until smooth.

Serve drizzled with olive oil and sprinkled with paprika.

Serves

10 as a dip

Ingredients

400 g can chickpeas, drained and rinsed
4 cloves of garlic, peeled
1 tbsp tahini
juice of 1 lemon
pinch of salt
pinch of chilli powder
3 tbsp olive oil
olive oil and paprika, to garnish

HERBED FALAFEL

A great companion to hummus, falafel is delicious, versatile, and tastes good hot or cold!

Method

Blitz the chickpeas and lemon juice in your food processor until nearly smooth. Add the rest of the ingredients and pulse until smooth and well-incorporated.

Using your hands, make the mixture into roughly tablespoon-sized balls, pressing together to keep firm.

Heat the oil in a deep frying pan over a medium heat, and fry the falafels – turn them halfway through, when they are becoming golden-brown.

Carefully remove the falafels from the oil and put them on kitchen paper to drain before enjoying on their own, dipped in delicious hummus, or in a wrap!

Feel free to change up the herbs you incorporate – mint can be a great addition!

Serves

4

Ingredients

2 x 400 g tins
    chickpeas, drained
    and rinsed
juice of 1 lemon
1 tbsp rose harissa,
    or to taste
1 tbsp tahini
½ tbsp allspice
1 large bunch
    of coriander
parsley, to taste
oil, for frying

GUACAMOLE

As a companion to tortilla chips, a topping for toast or as part of a Mexican-inspired wrap, guacamole is always the star of the show.

Method

Slice the avocados down the middle then twist the two halves to separate. Remove the stone, then chop each half in half again, vertically. The skin should easily peel back from the flesh at this point. Then chop the avocado into a large bowl.

Add the lime juice, and mash together until the avocado starts to become a smooth paste – you will want to leave a little texture.

Finely chop the jalapeños, deseed and finely chop the tomatoes, add in and stir through until mixed well. Sprinkle with the spices and serve.

Makes

1 large bowl

Ingredients

3 large ripe avocados
juice of 1 lime
jalapeños
2 large tomatoes
pinch of cayenne
    pepper
pinch of paprika

PESTO

This Italian classic packed with punchy basil gets its creaminess from pine nuts – simply delicious.

Method

In a heavy-bottomed frying pan, dry-fry the pine nuts over a low heat until they start to brown. Make sure to move them round the pan – either with a wooden spoon or by shaking.

Once the pine nuts are toasted, put them, together with the basil, olive oil, garlic and nutritional yeast, into your food processor and blitz until nice and smooth.

Store in a sterilised jar or serve straight away.

Makes

1 small jar — enough for 4 portions of well-coated pesto pasta

Ingredients

80 g pine nuts
130 g basil
150 ml extra virgin olive oil
4 cloves of garlic
nutritional yeast, to taste

ROOT VEGETABLE CRISPS

Why buy crisps by the bag when these crunchy delights are so simple to make? Serve on their own in all their colourful glory or paired with a dip.

Method

Wash all the veg, and top and tail them as needed, but leave the skins on if possible. Slice thinly, either by hand, or with a mandolin. Some graters can also be used to thinly slice.

In a deep frying pan, heat the oil over a medium heat and fry each vegetable type in batches. You may need to make several batches, as if you have too many in the pan at the same time they may stick together.

When they are crisp, and starting to curl, carefully remove from the oil and drain on kitchen paper.

Mix all the vegetable varieties together in your bowl, and sprinkle with a little salt.

Makes

1 large bowl
for sharing

Ingredients

2 beetroots
2 parsnips
2 carrots
1 sweet potato
oil, for frying
salt, to taste

KALE CRISPS

Kale is jam-packed with nutrients and is fantastic for your health, so it's already ticking a lot of boxes. Its ability to be easily transformed into a deliciously crispy, savoury snack just makes it even better!

Method

Preheat your oven to 180°C.

Wash the kale, then chop, removing the stems, into bite-sized pieces.

Arrange the kale onto a baking sheet and drizzle with olive oil. Go in with your hands and mix it up to make sure it is evenly coated. Sprinkle with salt and pepper, and bake in the oven until they start to turn golden at the edges – this is not an exact science so keep an eye on them!

When they are nearly done, sprinkle over sesame seeds and bake for the final 5 minutes. If you want even more punch, try using nutritional yeast, sliced garlic or garlic granules to season.

Makes

Enough for 2 to share

Ingredients

1 large head of kale
olive oil
salt
pepper
sesame seeds

Optional extras:
nutritional yeast
sliced garlic
garlic granules

LEMON AND THYME SWEET POTATO CRISPS

That sweet–savoury powerhouse, the sweet potato, is incredibly versatile. These simple-to-make crisps are a healthier way to indulge your potato snack cravings.

Method

Wash the sweet potatoes, but leave the skins on. Slice thinly, either by hand, or with a mandolin. Some graters can also be used to thinly slice.

In a large, deep frying pan, heat the oil over a medium heat and fry the sliced sweet potatoes in batches until crisp – turning halfway through. Remove them carefully from the oil, and drain on kitchen paper.

Put the crisps into a bowl and sprinkle liberally with the lemon zest, thyme, salt and pepper to achieve your perfect flavour balance.

Makes

Enough for 2 to share

Ingredients

large sweet potatoes
olive oil
the grated zest
   of 1 lemon
dried thyme
salt
pepper

CARAMEL POPCORN

Not just for the cinema, popcorn is a great snack to share. Don't be afraid of popping and seasoning it yourself – it's a lot easier than you might think.

Method

In a pan with a lid, heat the oil over a low–medium heat. When hot, add the popcorn to the oil, put the lid on, and swirl to coat all the kernels. Wait for the kernels to start popping, then swirl occasionally to avoid burning. When there is more than a second or two between pops, take off the heat and pour into your bowl.

For the caramel, melt the butter in a pan. Add the sugar, and heat gently until the sugar is fully dissolved and the mixture bubbles. Add the bicarb and salt and stir to incorporate.

You can either pour this mixture over the popcorn and leave it sticky, or put the popcorn onto a baking tray, pour the caramel over and bake for half an hour to really coat it.

Makes

1 large bowl of popcorn

Ingredients

coconut oil
30–50 g popping corn
100 g vegan butter
   substitute
120 g unrefined sugar
½ tsp bicarbonate
   of soda
pinch of salt

HOMEMADE OVEN-DRIED MANGO

Slightly crispy, chewy, sweet and satisfying, get your teeth into some slices of mango goodness.

Method

Preheat your oven to its lowest setting. Arrange the mango slices on a non-stick surface – a silicone baking mat is ideal.

Put them into the oven and bake for around 3 hours, making sure to regularly turn them so they dry out evenly. The exact time needed will depend on your oven, so keep an eye on them, particularly once they have been in for more than an hour, or they may become overly dry or burn.

Makes

A snack for 2

Ingredients

1 large mango, peeled,
  stone removed,
  and thinly sliced

FRUIT LEATHER

I know what you're saying – leather isn't vegan! But this kind is vegan, healthy and delicious! I've suggested apple and plum here, for quite an autumnal flavour, but lots of other flavour combinations would work too – so give it a go and experiment with your favourite fruits!

Method

Peel, core and chop the apples. Remove the stones from the plums and chop.

In a saucepan, heat the fruit with the water over a medium heat. When soft, add the sugar, and cook for around another 3 minutes. Transfer the mixture to your blender and blend until silky. Smooth the mixture out over a flat surface, such as a silicone baking mat. Take care to spread the mixture evenly along the surface, so that the finished fruit leather will have an even thickness.

Bake in your oven on its lowest setting for around 3 hours. The exact time will vary depending on your oven, so do check regularly. It will be ready when the mix feels slightly sticky to the touch, but does not come away on your finger.

Take the sheet out of the oven, and cut the finished fruit leather into strips. You can either leave it as is, or roll up!

Serves

4–6

Ingredients

4 medium apples
6 plums
120 ml water
2 tbsp sugar

CINNAMON AND MAPLE-ROASTED WALNUTS

Autumnal, fragrant and moreish, these roasted walnuts make a welcome change from the usual over-salted, shop-bought offerings.

Method

In a frying pan, cover the walnuts with the maple syrup and mix to ensure even coverage. Now add the other ingredients and mix well. If you have more of a sweet tooth, feel free to increase the sugar – the same with the cinnamon.

Transfer the pan to the hob and caramelise the nuts for 2–3 minutes, until golden brown. Allow to cool on baking paper before transferring to a bowl or jar.

Serves

2–4

Ingredients

170 g walnuts

70 ml maple syrup

2 tsp sugar

2 tsp cinnamon

SALT AND PEPPER ROASTED CHICKPEAS

Chickpeas: not just for hummus! They make a fantastic savoury snack when roasted – they are crispy and flavoursome.

Method

Dry the drained and rinsed chickpeas with kitchen paper. Transfer to a baking tray and toss with enough olive oil to coat, then sprinkle over the salt and pepper, mixing to ensure even coverage. Feel free to adjust the salt and pepper to your taste.

Roast in the oven at 180°C for around 25 minutes, until they start to turn a golden colour.

Allow to cool, and enjoy!

Serves

2–4

Ingredients

400 g can chickpeas, drained and rinsed
olive oil for roasting
1 tsp salt
2 tsp pepper

LIGHT BITES

Baked broccoli and kale sticks • Rice paper rolls with alfalfa sprouts • Sweet potato 'toast' • Beetroot burgers with guac • Pan-roasted mushrooms and sprouts • Jackfruit tacos • Chickpea salad jar • Buffalo cauliflower 'wings' • Tofu poké bowls • Baked aubergine bruschetta • Veggie kebabs • BBQ seitan sliders • Avocado tabbouleh • Chickpea and cauliflower 'mayo' flatbreads • Pitta pizza

BAKED BROCCOLI AND KALE STICKS

Broccoli and kale are both powerhouses of nutrition, and come together beautifully in these lightly fried bites. Pair them with your favourite salsa for delicious dipping.

Method

Prepare the green vegetables by washing them thoroughly and chopping them into small pieces. Steam the prepared vegetables for 5 minutes, or until they begin to get tender. Dice the onion finely and soften in a pan over a low–medium heat with a little oil.

In a large bowl, combine the vegetables, onion, garlic, chickpea flour, vegan cheese and seasoning, and mix well. The mixture should hold its shape when you come to fry it, so add a little more liquid if it's too dry, or add a little more chickpea flour if it's too wet.

Shape the mixture into wide sticks or sausages. In a deep frying pan, heat the oil, and then fry the sticks until golden on the outside, turning halfway through.

Remove carefully from the oil, then drain on kitchen paper before enjoying with your favourite salsa!

Serves

4

Ingredients

2 large heads
   of broccoli
1 large head of kale
1 small brown onion
4 cloves of garlic,
   minced
160 g chickpea flour
40 g vegan cheese
   (choose a
   parmesan- or
   cheddar-style
   cheese)
salt, pepper and chilli
   flakes, to taste
oil for shallow frying

RICE PAPER ROLLS WITH ALFALFA SPROUTS

Perfect paired with a peanut dipping sauce, these light, crispy rolls are fresh, summery and bursting with colour. The alfalfa sprouts add a wonderful crunch, and are highly nutritious.

Method

Peel the carrot and chop it into fine matchsticks – a mandolin is ideal for this. Chop the cucumber into matchsticks, and the peeled, de-stoned avocado into thin strips. Wash the mint.

Soak the rice paper wraps in cold water for 1–2 minutes, or according to the packet instructions.

One by one, build the wraps. Arrange the vegetables neatly in the centre of the rice paper, with 2 mint leaves (or more, to taste) in each, and the sprouts on top of the other vegetables. Roll up, then sprinkle with sesame seeds and enjoy with your favourite dipping sauce.

Makes

8 wraps

Ingredients

1 carrot
½ cucumber
1 avocado
16 large mint leaves
8 rice paper wraps
1 tub of alfalfa sprouts
black sesame seeds

SWEET POTATO 'TOAST'

As an alternative to bread-heavy treats, why not make a crostini-style bite with sweet potato bases? These flavoursome, filling bites boost your five a day, and look fantastic too! They will be softer than toast, so best eaten with a knife and fork...

Method

Preheat the oven to 200°C.

Wash the sweet potatoes, and slice them into rounds at least half an inch thick. Brush or rub the slices with the olive oil, and arrange onto baking trays. Sprinkle liberally with the seasonings – feel free to also season with your favourite herbs, if you like.

Roast in the oven for 25–30 minutes, or until golden.

Top with your favourite toppings – hummus is a great option (see p.31 for a tasty hummus recipe). I have gone for a smooth beetroot hummus, some fragrant chopped coriander and roasted chickpeas, but the options are endless!

Serves

4

Ingredients

2 large sweet potatoes
olive oil
salt, pepper, rosemary
    and thyme, to taste
toppings of your choice

BEETROOT BURGERS WITH GUAC

Try these beetroot and quinoa burgers for a healthy and delicious twist on a classic – it's far easier and faster than you might think.

Method

Peel and finely chop the onion. Remove the stem and seeds from the pepper and finely chop. Cook in a little oil for around 8 minutes – until the vegetables become less wet. Add the garlic and chopped coriander and cook for a further 1–2 minutes.

In your food processor, process half the black beans on a medium speed to form a dough. In a large bowl, add the processed and unprocessed beans, beetroot, quinoa, breadcrumbs, cooked vegetables and spices. Mix well so that the ingredients are evenly distributed.

Form the mixture into small patties – it will be sticky and thick at this point. Over a medium heat, preheat a little oil in a frying pan, then fry the patties, turning halfway through. Drain on kitchen paper before serving in a vegan charcoal bun, with salad leaves and plenty of fresh guacamole (see p.35).

Makes

8 burgers

Ingredients

1 medium red onion
1 red pepper
oil for frying
4 cloves of garlic, minced
1 large bunch
    of coriander
½ can black beans,
    drained and rinsed
1 beetroot, finely grated
175 g cooked quinoa
    (made according to the
    package instructions)
150 g breadcrumbs
1 tsp chilli flakes
1 tsp chilli powder
½ tsp smoked paprika
1 tbsp tapioca flour
charcoal buns
salad leaves
guacamole

PAN-ROASTED MUSHROOMS AND SPROUTS

Mushrooms and sprouts are a match made in heaven. Add salty soy and a little spice to the mix, and these become a joy. Pair them with some crusty bread or just enjoy them as they are.

Method

Take the outer leaves off of the sprouts, trim the bottoms, and wash, then cut in half vertically. Brush the mushrooms down with kitchen paper to remove dirt, then slice thickly.

Heat the oil in a deep frying pan over a medium heat. Add the halved sprouts, and cook until starting to soften. Add the garlic and cook for a further minute, then add the mushrooms.

When the mushrooms are soft and the sprouts are browning, add the soy sauce, pepper and chilli flakes, and cook for a further 1–2 minutes before serving with your choice of bread and topping with the chopped chives.

Serves

4

Ingredients

2 bags Brussels sprouts
2 large punnets
    chestnut mushrooms
olive oil, for pan frying
garlic puree or minced
    garlic, to taste
soy sauce, to taste
pepper, to taste
chilli flakes, to taste
chives, chopped

JACKFRUIT TACOS

Often referred to as 'vegan pulled pork', jackfruit is a versatile substitute for meat that absorbs flavours well, and is perfect for tacos!

Method

Drain the jackfruit in a colander, and rinse lightly. Use your fingers or a fork to break it down into shreds. In a bowl, mix the jackfruit with the seasonings – adjust to taste if you prefer a smokier taste (more smoked paprika), or a little more heat (more chilli powder). Cook gently in a pan over a medium heat, until it is warm through.

Serve in hard taco shells with all the trimmings – if you have the time, why not make your own fresh salsa and refried beans to go with the spicy jackfruit?

Serves

2–4

Ingredients

For the jackfruit:
1 can jackfruit
1 tbsp chilli powder
4 cloves of garlic, minced
1 tsp smoked paprika
1 tsp paprika
salt and pepper, to taste
oil for frying

To serve:
8 hard taco shells
shredded lettuce
vegan refried beans
vegan sour cream and/ or sriracha mayo
salsa

CHICKPEA SALAD JAR

Perfect as a larger snack on the go, or as part of a light lunch. Make this protein-topped salad in a mason jar and take it with you to work, to the beach, or just out into the garden on a warm day – bliss.

Method

Begin by peeling and grating the carrot, washing and slicing the cherry tomatoes, and washing the lettuce.

Start layering with the chickpeas, then add the carrot, the tomatoes, and the lettuce, letting each ingredient form a clear layer. Top with more of the chickpeas, and enjoy with your favourite salad dressing. I enjoy a vinaigrette made of 2 parts extra virgin olive oil to 1 part white wine vinegar, with a dash of wholegrain mustard and a little garlic puree – the acidity balances the flavours nicely.

Makes

1 jar – just multiply the ingredients for more servings

Ingredients

1 carrot
5 cherry tomatoes
1 handful of
    lamb's lettuce
¼ can chickpeas,
    drained and rinsed
dressing of your choice

BUFFALO CAULIFLOWER 'WINGS'

Buffalo 'wings' are delicious as a starter, or just as a snack shared with friends over a movie. These cauliflower 'wings' are full of flavour and definitely hit the spot.

Method

Preheat your oven to 200°C.

Prepare the cauliflower by washing well and cutting into florets.

In a large bowl, mix together the flour and spices, then add the water and soya milk. Mix well to form a thick batter – it should be thick enough to stick to the cauliflower.

Add the cauliflower to the bowl, and coat well with the batter. Transfer to non-stick and/or greased baking sheets, and bake for 20–30 minutes, until starting to turn golden.

In a pan, melt the vegan butter and add the hot sauce, mixing well. Then, remove the cauliflower from the oven, coat well with the spicy sauce and return to the oven to bake for around 10 minutes, until sticky.

Chop the green ends of the spring onions and scatter over your bowl to serve.

Serves

4

Ingredients

1 large or 2 small heads of cauliflower
250 g plain flour
2½ tsp garlic granules or powder (substitute for garlic puree if you prefer)
½ tsp ground cumin
½ tsp chilli powder
pinch of salt
pinch of pepper
1 tsp paprika
120 ml water
120 ml soya milk (unsweetened)
1 tbsp vegan butter substitute
200 ml hot sauce
2 spring onions

TOFU POKÉ BOWLS

Tofu is one of the cornerstones of vegan cooking – a powerful source of protein, it soaks up flavours beautifully and makes a gorgeous oriental-style meal in these pretty poké bowls.

Method

Drain and press the tofu – you may want to do this overnight for a really chewy, textured tofu.

Mix together the soy sauce, ginger and garlic, then put to one side.

Slice the tofu lengthways into 'steaks'. Marinate in the soy mixture until well-covered.

Make the rice noodles according to packet instructions.

Heat your oven to 180°C. Place the coated tofu onto a baking sheet, and bake in the oven for around 15–20 minutes, until starting to go golden and sticky.

Prepare the vegetables by heating through the edamame in a pan, or the microwave, slicing the cucumber and watermelon radish, and peeling the carrot then slicing it into ribbons with a mandolin or grater.

Fill 2 bowls with the rice noodles, then arrange the tofu, seaweed and vegetables on top. Use some extra soy-ginger dressing, or some sriracha on top, if desired.

Serves

2

Ingredients

1 block extra firm tofu
100 ml soy sauce
2 tbsp ginger paste
1 tbsp garlic paste
1 pack rice noodles
2 handfuls of
   edamame
¼ cucumber
1 watermelon radish
1 carrot
2 tbsp wakame
   seaweed

BAKED AUBERGINE BRUSCHETTA

Another great gluten-free recipe, this no-bread version of bruschetta is full of warmth and flavour.

Method

Preheat your oven to 180°C.

Wash the aubergines and cut off the stalks. Slice into thick slices, brush with olive oil, and bake in the oven for around 20 minutes, or until cooked through, turning halfway.

Deseed and chop the tomatoes, putting them into a large bowl. Peel and finely dice the onion and add to the tomato. Add the garlic, basil leaves (washed and torn), and drizzle with olive oil. Mix well, and season to taste.

Spoon even quantities of your tomato mixture onto the cooked aubergine, season and drizzle with good-quality balsamic vinegar.

Serves

4

Ingredients

2 large aubergines
olive oil
8 large tomatoes
1 small red onion
1 tsp garlic puree,
    or 1½ cloves of
    minced garlic
2 handfuls of fresh
    basil leaves
salt and pepper,
    to taste
balsamic vinegar,
    to drizzle

VEGGIE KEBABS

Not just for the barbecue, these veggie kebab skewers are rainbow-bright and nutrient-dense, whilst packing a real flavour punch.

Method

Lightly peel the courgettes, remove the stems, and cut into thick discs. Peel the onion, and cut into chunks. Wash, top and tail, and halve the radishes. De-stem and deseed the peppers, and cut into large chunks. Wash the tomatoes. Brush the mushrooms down with kitchen paper, then slice in half.

Arrange the vegetables on the skewers, making sure you have some of each kind per skewer, and varying the order. Brush or drizzle with olive oil, then cook on the barbecue, the grill, or in a griddle pan, until lightly charred.

Makes

8–10 skewers

Ingredients

2 courgettes
1 red onion
5 radishes
1 red and 1 yellow pepper
20 cherry tomatoes
20 mushrooms
olive oil, to drizzle

BBQ SEITAN SLIDERS

Sometimes known as 'wheat meat', seitan has a gluten base, and gives a deliciously chewy, textured meat substitute, perfect for these little sliders.

Method

To make the seitan, mix the dry ingredients together, then add the soy and barbecue sauces. Add up to two-thirds of the stock gradually, mixing well, until a stiff dough is formed with no dry patches. Knead thoroughly.

In a large saucepan, keep the remaining stock on a simmer. Add the chilli flakes, molasses, and pepper.

Press the seitan dough and then slice into rounded 'steaks'. They should be slightly smaller than you want the finished 'steaks' to be, as they will swell.

Add the 'steaks' to the stock pan – you may have to do this in batches. Simmer them for around 30 minutes, turning occasionally and making sure they don't stick together. They should float to the surface when ready.

Drain the 'steaks'. Heat the oil in a griddle pan, and fry the seitan on each side, until it is starting to crisp. Serve in rolls of your choice with shredded lettuce and barbecue sauce, ketchup, cheese, or vegan mayo.

Makes

10 sliders

Ingredients

510 g vital wheat gluten, measured out in cups or a jug
35 g nutritional yeast
1 tbsp dark brown sugar
½ tsp smoked paprika
2 tsp garlic granules or powder
2 tsp onion granules or powder
¼ tsp chilli powder
vegetable stock – enough for a large pot
1 tbsp soy sauce
3 tbsp barbecue sauce
chilli flakes, to taste
1 tbsp molasses
pepper, to taste
oil, for frying

AVOCADO TABBOULEH

In a fresh take on tabbouleh, try this avocado-based salad – great on its own, it also makes a perfect accompaniment to some of the other delicious dishes in this chapter, such as the sliders, or kebabs.

Method

Rinse the bulgur wheat. Once the water runs clear, place the drained wheat into a bowl. Cover with 200 ml of boiling water, cover the bowl with a tea towel, and set aside for around half an hour.

Wash and roughly chop the herbs. Place them in a large bowl. Wash and chop the cherry tomatoes and add them to the herbs. Prepare the avocados as on p.35, then chop the avocado into your bowl.

Drain the bulgur wheat, and add it to your waiting herbed salad. Mix well, then dress with the lemon juice and olive oil and top with sumac and the chopped spring onions.

Serves

2

Ingredients

50 g bulgur wheat
50 g flat-leaf parsley
50 g mint
175 g cherry tomatoes
2 large ripe avocados
juice of 1 lemon
4 tbsp olive oil
sumac
spring onions, chopped

CHICKPEA AND CAULIFLOWER 'MAYO' FLATBREADS

Flatbreads make a versatile snack, and this savoury combination of roasted cauliflower, chickpeas and vegan garlic mayo on a base of smashed avocado is unusual and full of flavour.

Method

Preheat your oven to 180°C. First, wash the cauliflower and cut it into florets. Drain and rinse the chickpeas thoroughly.

Place the cauliflower on a non-stick baking tray, drizzle with the olive oil and roast in the oven for 30 minutes, or until cooked through, and starting to brown. About 5–10 minutes before the cauliflower is due to come out of the oven, add the chickpeas and roast.

Prepare the avocados as for guacamole (p.35), chopping into a large bowl. Add the lemon juice and crush the avocado with a fork.

Build each flatbread by starting with a layer of avocado, then adding the cauliflower, then chickpeas, and topping with garlic mayo to taste.

Serves

4

Ingredients

1 head of cauliflower
400 g can chickpeas
olive oil, to drizzle
2 large ripe avocados
lemon juice, to taste
vegan garlic mayo
4 flatbreads

PITTA PIZZA

So much better than the mini pizzas you can buy in the supermarket, and just as quick to make, pitta pizzas are super versatile! Try the toppings suggested here as your starting point, then go all out with your favourite flavours for a properly-personalised pizza.

Method

Preheat your oven to 180°C.

Prepare the vegetables by washing and slicing them.

Spread each pitta with passata. Top with vegan cheese, grated or in slices. Add the sliced black olives, pepper pieces, cherry tomato slices and red onion.

Season to taste.

Bake in the oven for 5–10 minutes, then slice into wedges and enjoy!

Serves

6

Ingredients

sliced black olives
1 red pepper
6 cherry tomatoes
¼ red onion
6 pittas
passata
vegan cheese, such
    as Violife
salt
pepper

AFTERNOON TREATS

Berry muffins • Fruity ice pops • Truffles • Coconut cream tarts • Chocolate coconut bites • Peanut brittle • Classic banana bread • Apple pie milkshake • Creamy coconut-milk iced coffee • Pistachio and goji berry brownies • Chocolate chip cookie dough

BERRY MUFFINS

Muffins are delicious any time of the day, and particularly good for afternoon tea! These fluffy berry muffins have extra goodness from oats too – sweet!

Method

Preheat your oven to 180°C.

In a small bowl or jug, whisk together the soya milk and vinegar, then set aside.

In a medium bowl, sift together the flour and bicarbonate of soda.

In a large bowl, whisk the oil and sugar together until they resemble caramel. Add the vanilla and almond extracts, then add the soya mixture and mix well.

Add the dry ingredients to the wet in 2 or 3 batches, combining thoroughly.

Add the berries, mixing through to make sure they are evenly distributed. Take care not to over-mix and knock the air out of the batter, though.

Spoon the mixture into muffin cases in a deep muffin tin, then sprinkle with the oats. Bake for around half an hour, or until they have risen and are golden. Cool on a wire rack.

Makes

12 muffins

Ingredients

310 ml soya milk
2 tbsp cider vinegar
900 g plain white flour
2 tsp bicarbonate
    of soda
175 ml light oil,
    such as rapeseed
350 g golden
    caster sugar
2 tbsp vanilla extract
1 tsp almond extract
4 handfuls of fresh
    or frozen berries
    – try blueberries,
    raspberries and
    strawberries
oats, to top

FRUITY ICE POPS

These are so fun to make! Once you get an ice-pop mould and start experimenting, the delicious combinations are endless! Below is a recipe for berry pops, and some more flavour suggestions.

Method

Whisk up the coconut milk until it is smooth and the cream is well distributed.

Blitz the berries and vanilla extract in your blender or food processor.

Mix the berries into the coconut milk, then pour into your mould.

Freeze for half an hour, then insert your lolly sticks.

Freeze for at least another 4 hours, but check to see when firm, as they may need longer.

WHY NOT TRY...

Chocolate and pistachio

Avocado—lime

Blood orange

Blueberry

Strawberry—banana

Makes

Enough to fill 4 regular ice-pop moulds

Ingredients

400 g can coconut milk

200 g strawberries

100 g raspberries

½ tsp vanilla extract

TRUFFLES

So, you thought you couldn't make truffles without dairy? Think again! These delicious, creamy confections are versatile, and quick to make too!

Method

Break up the chocolate into a heatproof bowl.

In a small pan, gently heat the coconut milk.

Pour the coconut milk over the chocolate, stirring gently as you go. Add the vanilla, and continue to stir gently until fully combined.

Cover the bowl, and put in the fridge for at least 4 hours to set.

Once set, use a spoon to scoop out chunks of the mix, which you can roll in your palms to shape. You can then roll these in cocoa powder, if you wish, especially if your mix has come out sticky. Either way, then roll some in the coconut, some in the pistachios, and some in the hazelnuts for a trio of tempting chocolate treats.

Makes

Around 20 truffles

Ingredients

150 g good quality dark chocolate
110 ml coconut milk
dash of vanilla extract
desiccated coconut, crushed pistachios, and toasted crushed hazelnuts, to coat

COCONUT CREAM TARTS

Creamy, fresh, decadent and delicious – these little tarts are like a slice of summer.

Method

Preheat the oven to 180°C.

Grease tartlet cases or a tartlet tin with vegan margarine. Line the cases with the pastry, prick the base all over, and blind bake for 15 minutes. To do this, line the pastry case with baking paper, and fill with baking beans (these are usually ceramic, and can be bought in cookware shops), or with dry rice. Once you have done this, and removed your baking beans or rice, bake for another 5 minutes until golden, then remove from the oven and set aside to cool.

Whip the coconut cream with the sugar and vanilla until it forms stiff peaks. If it is staying too runny, adding a little more sugar and/or some tapioca flour can help.

Spoon the cream into the cooled cases – you may have some left over. Chill in the fridge for another 30 minutes or so, before topping with fresh berries to serve.

Makes

6 tarts

Ingredients

vegan margarine, to grease the tin

2 rolls of ready-made vegan shortcrust pastry, such as Jus-Rol

400 ml coconut cream (not coconut milk or creamed coconut), chilled

60 g icing sugar

3 tsp vanilla extract

fresh raspberries and blueberries, to top

CHOCOLATE COCONUT BITES

These treats taste like that famous chocolate bar, but with less sugar, less fat, and no animal products – perfect for sharing on movie night, or with coffee.

Method

In your food processor, pulse the coconut until it resembles coarse salt. Transfer to a bowl, and add the maple syrup, coconut oil and vanilla extract – stir to combine.

Using your hands, roll the mixture together to form slightly elongated balls – like little bars. You may need to apply some pressure to squash the mixture together to ensure they hold their shape. Place in the fridge to cool and harden for at least half an hour.

Melt the chocolate in a heatproof bowl, over a pan of boiling water, stirring continuously as it melts. Dip your coconut centres in the chocolate, rolling to ensure even coverage, then place on greaseproof paper. Once they are all covered, place the chocolate bites into the fridge to cool and harden. Once hardened, they are also best stored in the fridge, but can be stored in a box with a lid, rather than on a flat tray.

Makes

12 bites

Ingredients

600 g desiccated coconut
2–3 tbsp maple syrup
4 tbsp virgin coconut oil
1 tsp vanilla extract
120 g dark chocolate

PEANUT BRITTLE

This just makes me think of my childhood – peanut brittle is by no means a healthy choice, but it tastes fantastic, and homemade is even better!

Method

Grease a baking tray with a lip – a flat baking tray would allow the caramel to run off, which we want to avoid.

In a saucepan, melt together the sugar, margarine and salt, and bring to the boil for around 5 minutes, or until the mixture has completely caramelised. Make sure you stir throughout to avoid burning, and ensure no sugar crystals remain.

Arrange the peanuts onto the greased tray, and pour the caramel over them evenly. Allow to cool before either cutting with a hot knife, or smashing into shards.

Makes

1 tray

Ingredients

100 g vegan margarine, plus more for greasing
200 g caster sugar
pinch of salt
300 g peanuts

CLASSIC BANANA BREAD

The classic teatime loaf, banana bread is beautifully squidgy, and sweet–savoury – enjoy it as is, or toast it and spread with vegan butter for a warm slice of indulgence.

Method

Preheat your oven to 180°C, and grease a loaf tin.

Peel and chop the bananas into a large mixing bowl, then cream together with the sugar, margarine and vanilla until fairly smooth – some lumps are good as these will form delicious, moist pockets of fruit.

In a separate bowl, mix together the flour, baking powder and cinnamon. Now, add the dry ingredients to the wet in 2 batches, folding through, before pouring the mixture into the greased loaf tin. If you wish to, halve a banana and lay it on top as a decorative addition – it will bake into the loaf.

Bake for around 30 minutes, or until it has risen and is a golden colour. Allow to cool a little in the tin, before turning out and cooling on a wire rack.

Makes

1 loaf

Ingredients

50 g vegan margarine, plus extra for greasing
4 large overripe bananas
120 g golden caster sugar
1 tsp vanilla extract
225 g plain flour
3 tsp baking powder
1 tsp cinnamon

APPLE PIE MILKSHAKE

All the flavours of apple pie in a cool, milky drink?
Yes please!

Method

First, prepare your apples by peeling and chopping them.
Add them to a saucepan with the sugar and one third of
the cinnamon and nutmeg, to stew.

Shake together the non-dairy milk, remaining spices,
vanilla extract and maple syrup, until the milk is frothy
and the spices well distributed.

Divide between 2 glasses, and top with some of the
stewed apple and a sprinkling of cinnamon.

For a thicker shake, blend the milk with 2 tablespoons of
vanilla dairy-free ice cream, and some of the stewed apple
– delicious!

Serves

2 – multiply
ingredients for
more servings

Ingredients

2 tart apples
25 g sugar
1½ tsp cinnamon
¾ tsp nutmeg
700 ml soya or
    oat milk
½ tsp vanilla extract
maple syrup, to taste

CREAMY COCONUT-MILK ICED COFFEE

A fantastic pick-me-up for a warm day, iced coffee is one of my favourite things. This coconut milk version has a beautiful nutty undertone that pairs well with caramel- or chocolate-noted coffees.

Method

First, brew your coffee. Pour the brewed coffee over ice – as most glasses are not heatproof, I suggest doing this in a jug first (or a cup if you don't have a jug to hand), and then transferring into your glasses.

Shake up/mix the coconut milk well, making sure the cream is well distributed. Add to the coffee and ice, along with agave nectar or maple syrup for sweetness. At this point, you could also add a little flavouring, such as vanilla or chocolate extract.

Put more ice into your glasses, and divide the creamy coffee mixture evenly.

Makes

2 large glasses — multiply ingredients for more servings

Ingredients

500 ml fresh
   brewed coffee
ice cubes
500 ml coconut milk
agave nectar or maple
   syrup, to taste

PISTACHIO AND GOJI BERRY BROWNIES

Full of goodness, these rich chocolate brownies are fantastic with coffee, and are ideal for taking with you for an afternoon snack when out and about. Did I mention they are gluten-free, too?

Method

Preheat the oven to 180°C, and grease your brownie tin.

Put all the ingredients except the coconut oil, goji berries and pistachios into a large bowl, and mix well to combine.

Slowly add the coconut oil to the mixture – it may form clumps so be sure to mix well to keep smooth.

Fold in the goji berries and pistachios, ensuring they are evenly distributed, then pour the mixture into your brownie tin and smooth the top.

Bake for around 25 minutes, or until the tip of a sharp knife comes out clean after insertion. The finished brownies should be fudgy and chewy.

Makes

12 brownies

Ingredients

200 g apple sauce (smooth and unsweetened)

75 g golden caster sugar

25 g good quality cocoa powder

100 g gluten-free plain white flour blend

¼ tsp xanthan gum

pinch of sea salt

¼ tsp bicarbonate of soda

50 g coconut oil, melted

30 g goji berries, softened in water and drained

30 g chopped pistachios

CHOCOLATE CHIP COOKIE DOUGH

Always want to lick the bowl? Now you can! Try this cookie dough, which is safe to eat raw, and you may never get as far as baking the cookies again!

Method

In a large bowl, mix together all the ingredients, except the chocolate chips, mixing well until a dough is formed.

Fold in the chocolate chips and enjoy!

Makes

1 bowl – to share!

Ingredients

100 g almond flour (if you can't find this, make it at home by blitzing almonds in your food processor)

50 g coconut flour

3 tbsp coconut oil

4–5 tbsp agave or date nectar – depending how sweet you want it!

3 tsp vanilla extract or vanilla paste

pinch of sea salt

100 g dark chocolate chips

AFTER-DINNER INDULGENCES

Quick berry n'ice cream • Fruit sorbets • Fudgy flapjacks • Chocolate–avocado mousse • Matcha tea and lime pie • Zesty orange cake • Strawberry cheesecake • Deep dark chocolate fondue

QUICK BERRY N'ICE CREAM

Made with a banana base, this naughty-but-nice indulgence is far healthier than traditional ice cream. Quick to make, and totally delicious, it's the perfect dessert for a hot day!

Method

For best results, have a stash of frozen berries and banana slices ready to blitz. This recipe is better eaten fresh than after being stored in the freezer, so get ready to indulge!

In your food processor, blitz together the frozen fruit and coconut milk until smooth. Add a little agave nectar for extra sweetness if desired.

Once smooth and thick, put into bowls and serve!

Serves

2

Ingredients

2 frozen, sliced bananas

2 handfuls of frozen mixed berries

60 ml coconut milk or cream

FRUIT SORBETS

Zesty, tangy, sweet and cool, sorbet is a beautiful and delicate way to end a meal – why not try experimenting with your favourite flavours?

Method

This is a very simple (dare I say 'cheat'?) way to make sorbet, with very little added sugar, and without the need for an ice cream maker or the constant mixing and refreezing many recipes call for.

The flavours I've suggested are: 'Mango', 'Blueberry', and 'Honeydew melon, lemon and lime'. Quite simply, you chop up fresh fruit (no need to chop the blueberries), then freeze it. Once frozen, you blitz it in your food processor for a healthy, delicious snack or after-dinner treat.

With the lemon and lime that goes into the melon flavour, juice them and add to taste, rather than freezing – though you can freeze the juice and use this. Add agave nectar, to taste, to sweeten these while blitzing.

Makes

As much as you'd like to eat or share

Ingredients

Fruit!
agave nectar, to taste

For these flavours:
Mango
Blueberries
Honeydew melon,
    lemons, limes

FUDGY FLAPJACKS

What could make a flapjack even tastier? A fudgy, nutty topping! Enjoy these gooey treats at your peril – you may not be able to stop at just one!

Method

Preheat your oven to 180°C. Grease a baking tin with a lip.

In a pan over a medium heat, melt together the margarine, sugar and syrup until the sugar is fully incorporated and there are no clumps.

In a bowl, mix the sugar mixture with the oats until the oats are well coated, then transfer to the baking tray and press flat, ensuring even thickness. Bake in the oven for around 30 minutes, then allow to cool in the tin

To make the topping, put all the ingredients into your food processor except the pumpkin seeds, and pulse until smooth and caramel-like. Add a little water if the mixture looks too thick, and vary the amount of maple syrup if you prefer more/less sweetness.

Once the flapjacks have cooled, spread the fudgy topping over them evenly, smoothing the top. Sprinkle with the pumpkin seeds, and chop into little squares to serve.

Makes

1 tray

Ingredients

For the flapjack:
180 g non-dairy
   margarine
130 g golden
   caster sugar
1½ tbsp agave nectar
   or golden syrup
360 g porridge oats

For the fudgy topping:
110 g pitted dates,
   chopped
40 g ground almonds
pinch of salt
2 tbsp maple syrup
pumpkin seeds

CHOCOLATE-AVOCADO MOUSSE

Avocados? In a dessert? Yes! Full of good fats, avocados are perfect for creamy, mousse-like desserts (or indeed, mousse) and pair really well with chocolate.

Method

Prepare the avocados as per p.35. Chop the avocado into your food processor, then add all the ingredients except the chocolate. Blitz until smooth.

In a heatproof bowl, melt the chocolate over a pan of water on a medium heat. Once melted, add the chocolate to the mixture and blitz again until well combined.

Transfer the mixture to ramekins or glasses, smooth it over and chill in the freezer until fully set – at least 2 hours.

Before serving, get out of the freezer and leave to soften for 5 minutes or so. Top with chopped hazelnuts and sliced strawberries, or your favourite toppings.

If there's any left over, store, covered, in the freezer.

Serves

4

Ingredients

3 small ripe avocados
80 ml non-dairy milk — soya or almond work well
4 tbsp maple syrup
1 tbsp almond butter
1 tbsp arrowroot
pinch of salt
2 tsp vanilla extract
25 g cocoa powder
175 g chocolate for melting, such as chocolate chips or baking chocolate

MATCHA TEA AND LIME PIE

Green tea gives incredible colour and flavour – with avocados for silky smoothness and the tang of lime, this creamy raw pie will leave you wanting more.

Method

For the base, soften all the ingredients (except the salt) in warm water for 5 minutes or so, then drain and blitz, together with the salt, in your food processor. Press this mixture firmly into a tart case, to form a good, firm base for your filling. Chill in the fridge while you make your filling.

For the filling, first melt the coconut oil, and put aside. Next prepare the avocados as per p.35, then chop them into your food processor. Add the remaining ingredients, and pulse until smooth and well combined. Add the coconut oil and pulse again until fully mixed.

Transfer the filling to your chilled crust, and chill overnight, or for at least 3 hours.

To serve, decorate with the raspberries and coconut.

Makes

1 pie

Ingredients

For the base:
75 g walnuts
75 g almonds
4 tbsp flax seeds
100 g pitted dates
pinch of salt

For the filling:
75 g coconut oil, melted
3 large ripe avocados
grated zest of 2 limes,
    and juice of 1
3 tbsp agave nectar,
    or to taste
2 tbsp matcha tea
    powder

To serve:
fresh raspberries
coconut shavings

ZESTY ORANGE CAKE

Loaf cakes are a great dessert for a dinner party, as they feed so many without too much effort! The delicious orange flavour pairs well with a chocolate sauce, or with vanilla non-dairy ice cream for extra indulgence.

Method

Preheat your oven 180°C. Grease a loaf tin with vegan spread.

Put the milk into a small bowl and add the cider vinegar – whisk until frothy and set aside.

In a large bowl, mix together the flour, baking powder and sugar.

Add the oil, orange zest and juice to the milk mixture, stirring it through, then add the wet ingredients to the dry in 2 batches, stirring to incorporate well.

Pour the cake mix into the baking tin and bake in the oven for around 45 minutes, or until risen, golden, and the tip of a knife comes out clean when inserted. Allow to cool first in the tin, and then on a wire rack.

You may wish to decorate with orange slices before baking, or make a drizzle to go over the cake once baked – either would add a little something extra.

Makes

1 cake

Ingredients

vegan margarine
   for greasing
250 ml soya milk,
   or other non-dairy
   milk (almond
   also works well)
1 tbsp cider vinegar
250 g plain flour
2 tsp baking powder
175 g golden
   caster sugar
70 ml light oil such
   as rapeseed
zest of 1–2 oranges,
   depending how
   strong you'd like the
   zesty flavour to be
4 tbsp freshly squeezed
   orange juice

STRAWBERRY CHEESECAKE

A dessert to remind you of childhood, but with far more goodness – from the real fruit in the creamy topping to the nutty base – this one is a real winner.

Method

Soak the nuts for the base for at least 3 hours. In a separate bowl, soak the cashews for your cheesecake.

Thoroughly drain and blitz the nuts for your base in your food processor, together with the dates – this should look similar to crushed biscuits. Press this mixture into the bottom of your pie dish and chill.

For the cheesecake, take the drained cashews and process with the vanilla bean paste in your food processor until smooth – you may need to add some coconut water to help thin this out. Melt the coconut oil in a heatproof bowl over a pan of boiling water, and add to the cashew mix along with agave nectar and lemon juice. Process until combined and very smooth.

Blend two thirds of the strawberries with half the cashew mixture, keeping the other half of the cashew mixture aside to be plain vanilla. Layer the two flavours of cheesecake, vanilla first, then strawberry, onto the base. Top with the remaining strawberries, and chill until ready to serve.

Makes

1 large cheesecake,
or 8 small ones

Ingredients

For the base:
75 g almonds
75 g cashews
100 g chopped
   pitted dates

For the cheesecake:
250 g cashews
1 tsp vanilla bean paste
coconut water, as
   needed
75 g coconut oil
75 ml agave nectar
1½ tbsp lemon juice
325 g fresh
   strawberries,
   de-stemmed

DEEP DARK CHOCOLATE FONDUE

Simply delicious – sumptuous, liquid chocolate-dipped bites that are a perfect way to end a meal.

Method

Break up or chop the chocolate into fine pieces, and place in a heatproof bowl.

Heat the milk in a saucepan over a low heat, until near boiling. Add the salt. Remove the milk from the heat and pour over the chocolate, ensuring that all pieces are fully covered.

Cover the bowl and set aside for 3–5 minutes.

Add the vanilla, and the liqueur (if using), to the chocolate mixture and whisk to combine well.

Serve immediately with your choice of dippables – fruit such as strawberries, or more indulgent treats such as pieces of cake or vegan marshmallows – enjoy!

Makes

1 pot

Ingredients

For the fondue:
225 g dark chocolate
300 ml soya or
   oat milk
pinch of sea salt
1 tsp vanilla extract
liqueur of choice
   (optional)

**Suggestions
for dipping:**
strawberries
blueberries
grapes
vegan marshmallows
cake pieces

If you're interested in finding out more about our books,
find us on Facebook at *Summersdale Publishers*
and follow us on Twitter at *@summersdale*.

www.summersdale.com

Image credits